EVEN IF YOU CAN'T CARRY A TUNE...

GRAMMAR THROUGH POPULAR SONGS

By Polly Merdinger and Joel Rosenfeld

NEWBURY HOUSE PUBLISHERS, Cambridge
A division of Harper & Row, Publishers, Inc.
New York, Philadelphia, San Francisco, Washington
London, Mexico City, São Paulo, Singapore, Sydney

1984

Library of Congress Cataloging in Publication Data

Merdinger, Polly.
    Even if you can't carry a tune.

    1. English language--Text-books for foreign speakers.
2. English language--Grammar--1950–   .   3. Music in
education.   I. Rosenfeld, Joel.   II. Title.
PE1128.M44   1984   428.2'4   84-8367
ISBN 0-88377-465-8

NEWBURY HOUSE PUBLISHERS
A division of Harper & Row, Publishers, Inc.

Language Science
Language Teaching
Language Learning

CAMBRIDGE, MASSACHUSETTS

First printing: September 1984

Printed in the U.S.A.   3 4   5   6 7 8 9 10

We dedicate this book to
Ruth, Julius and David Merdinger
and Gail Rosenfeld

Acknowledgments

We would like to express our appreciation to our students and colleagues at the American Language Program of Columbia University for all of their encouragement. We would especially like to thank Lou Levi and Mary Jerome for their constant support, and for being there when we needed them. Special thanks to Mary Colonna for her valuable feedback and suggestions.

Mark Rosenfeld was of invaluable help to us in selecting the songs for this book. Thanks to Linda Ferreira for all her help, especially in the planning stages of the book, and to Artie Cohen for helping us with the production of the cassette.

Jim Brown, our editor at Newbury House, believed in our project from the start, and was a tremendous source of encouragement and advice. For his active participation in discussions ranging from English grammar to the latest Islanders' game, we thank him.

Polly Merdinger would like to thank Bronx House Emanuel Camp, where music and singing became an important part of her life.

Joel Rosenfeld would like to thank Gail Rosenfeld for her unwavering support and love throughout the creation of this text.

Introduction

Even if you can't carry a tune, you may still be a music lover. Just as we love bringing music into our own lives, as ESL (English as a Second Language) teachers we enjoy sharing music with our students.

The use of songs in ESL is not new. A lot of material has been designed using popular songs to teach vocabulary, or for discussion purposes. Those songs which were designed to teach grammar were always written or rewritten by ESL teachers for ESL students.

We have tried to bridge these two approaches. We believe that in addition to their cultural value, popular songs are a very effective means for teaching grammar in a natural context. We have carefully selected well known songs of various musical styles, which clearly illustrate grammatical structures and their functions.

This book is intended for beginning through intermediate students. You will notice, however, that the themes of the units are sophisticated ones, not usually dealt with in beginning level texts. Don't be put off by what look like difficult vocabulary and discussion topics. You will find that the students become highly motivated to learn the related vocabulary and use the structures embedded in the songs.

After an initial section on listening comprehension, each unit moves from highly structured exercises to very free ones. Each unit is thematically related to the song and the grammatical function presented.

We have used this material extensively with great success. Students become very enthusiastic; there is a lot of foot tapping, humming along, and general involvement as the songs are played.

Music is an important part of every culture. Even an unfamiliar song may be welcomed by an ESL student for whom music is a natural and familiar mode of expression. Using this material will open up the world of American music to students who otherwise might not know where to begin.

Notes to the Teacher

The material in *Even If You Can't Carry a Tune* can be used to present or reinforce and practice grammatical structures. Nine grammatical points are presented as well as a final integration chapter. You can use the chapters in any order—the chapters are not interdependent. However, the level of vocabulary of the last two chapters is higher than the others.

Each unit consists of these sections:

Song Introduction
Listening Comprehension
Song Task
Grammar Function
Structured Practice 1 / Structured Practice 2
Vocabulary
Discussion and Writing
Understanding the Structures (optional; to be found in back of book)

The section titled **Understanding the Structures** is found in the back of the book. This section is for students who need extra clarification of the particular structure (its use and form) before going on to **Structured Practice**. The complete lyrics to each of the songs can also be found in this section.

Before using this material for the first time, we often speak to the class about the value of songs as a tool for learning English. Here is the way we use the material.

To begin each chapter, we have students read **Song Introduction**, or it can be read by the teacher as a dictation. The introduction is intended to set the scene and give an idea of what is to come.

At the beginning of each chapter, there are three listening comprehension questions to test the students' understanding of the main points of the song. We ask the students to read the statements before listening to the song so that they have an idea of what information to listen for. We have deliberately used the choices TRUE/NOT TRUE (rather than TRUE/FALSE) because we feel that the resulting statements ("that's true," "that's not true") will more closely resemble natural language.

We then play the song. While some students find it a challenge to listen to a song for the first time without looking at the lyrics, other students may find it frustrating. You can decide whether or not to show them the lyrics at this stage. However, if they do look at the words at this stage, you should remind them not to do **Song Task**. The students do not have to understand every word but they must have a general understanding of the song before going on to the next exercise. Because the songs have not been altered or simplified in any way, many of them contain idiomatic and poetic expressions. These, as well as any difficult words, have been glossed next to the lyrics.

Once you and the class are satisfied that the song has been understood, we change our focus from general understanding to more specific tasks. In **Song Task**, students are asked to do a particular task. The tasks vary with each chapter. We usually play the song twice (or more if necessary) to complete this exercise. In most cases, **Song Task** is designed to help students focus on the structure being presented.

In **Grammar Function**, we have provided a clear and concise explanation of the function of the structure that is presented in the theme of the chapter. For example, "following the crowd" is the theme of the chapter on the simple present tense. The simple present tense is naturally elicited in the song *Little Boxes*.

Since this book is intended as a supplement, we assume that the students have already been introduced to the structures being presented. However, if you feel your students need a more basic understanding of the structure, you should at this point turn to the section titled **Understanding the Structures**, which is found in the back of the book. In this section, we have provided basic exercises and explanations to aid students in recognizing and understanding the structures.

The next two exercises are designed to help students test their understanding of the structure and practice their use of it. **Structured Practice 1** is more controlled (usually a cloze). **Structured Practice 2** is much less controlled and allows the student a great deal of freedom. Because the theme is functionally related, the grammar being presented will be naturally elicited, even in this freer practice exercise.

In **Vocabulary**, we have provided a list of words which are useful in the free practice and discussion and writing sections. Following the list is a vocabulary exercise in which students are asked to select the correct word in sentence level contexts.

We end each chapter with **Discussion and Writing**. Most of the questions are designed to elicit naturally the grammar being presented. These questions can be used in class or can be assigned as homework.

We always end our classes by playing the song again and encouraging the students to sing along.

Contents

1. Heartbreak

Tennessee Waltz

Grammar Focus Past continuous tense

Grammar Function Narrating a past event, storytelling

Song Introduction *The Tennessee Waltz* tells a sad story of love and heartbreak. It is a popular example of American country music, and it is well known all over the world.

Listening Comprehension Listen to the song and decide if the following statements are TRUE or NOT TRUE.

1. _____ The narrator and his girlfriend danced together the whole evening.

2. _____ He met a stranger at the party.

3. _____ The narrator's girlfriend left him.

1

Song Task   Listen to the song. Underline the correct form of the verb in parentheses. Choose between the past and past continuous tenses. Choose "when" or "while" where indicated.

Tennessee Waltz*
by Redd Stewart and Pee Wee King

1   I (waltzed/was waltzing) with my darling
2   To the Tennessee Waltz,
3   (When/While) an old friend I (happened/was happening) to see.
4   I (introduced/was introducing) him to my darling
5   And (when/while) they (danced/were dancing),
6   That friend (stole/was stealing) my sweetheart from me.

7   Yes, I remember the night and the Tennessee Waltz,
8   Only you know how much I have lost.
9   (When/While) I (lost/was losing) my little darling
10 The night they (played/were playing)
11 That beautiful Tennessee Waltz.

12 Yes, I remember the night and the Tennessee Waltz,
13 Only you know how much I have lost.
14 (When/While) I (lost/was losing) my little darling
15 The night they (played/were playing)
16 That beautiful Tennessee Waltz.

*TENNESSEE WALTZ by Redd Stewart and Pee Wee King © Copyright 1948, Renewed 1975 by Acuff-Rose Publications, Inc. Used by permission of the Publisher. All Rights Reserved. International Copyright Secured. Made in U.S.A.

Grammar Function

We use the past continuous tense for two purposes:

When two or more actions happen at the same time in the past *AND* it's not exactly clear when the actions began or ended, we use the past continuous tense for both verbs.

Example: While I was dancing with my girlfriend, the band was playing the Tennessee Waltz.

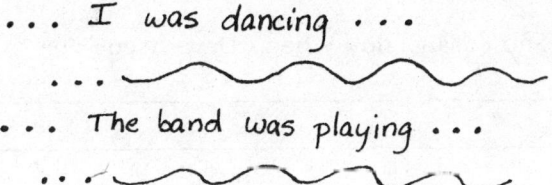

When one action interrupts another in the past, we use the past continuous tense to describe the action that is interrupted and the simple past tense for the interruption.

Example: While I was dancing with my girlfriend, I saw an old friend.

See also *Understanding the Structures,* p. 79.

Structured Practice 1   *Directions:*   Form complete questions from the words below. Use only the simple past and past continuous tenses.

Example: What / the band / play / when / Joe / steal / Susan ?

Question: *What was the band playing when Joe stole Susan?*

Answer: *The band was playing the Tennessee Waltz when Joe stole Susan.*

1. What / Dave and Susan / do / when / Dave / see / Joe ?

Question: _____

Answer: _____

2. When / Joe / notice / Susan / what / the band / play ?

Question: _____

Answer: _____

3. When / Dave / see / Joe / what / he / do ?

Question: _____

Answer: _____

4. Whom / Dave / see / while / he / dance / with Susan ?

Question: _____

Answer: _____

5. What / the band / play / while / Dave and Susan / dance ?

Question: _____

Answer: _____

Structured Practice 2 Imagine that you are Dave or Susan or Joe. It is the day after the dance and you are describing last night's events to a friend.

Dave   Susan   Joe

Vocabulary   Here are some words that may be useful in your discussion and writing.

to stare at—(verb) to look at steadily
to glare at—(verb) to look at in an angry way
to flirt with—(verb) to try to get romantic interest from another person
to fall in love with—(idiom) to begin to feel love for another person
to notice—(verb) to pay attention to
to break someone's heart—(idiom) to make someone very sad
heartbroken—(adjective) having hurt feelings, very sad
by chance—(idiom) by accident; not planned

Vocabulary Exercise   In the sentences below, fill in the blanks with the correct word or expression from the list above. (You may have to change the form—singular to plural, for example.)

1. After Joe and Susan left the party, Dave was alone. He felt angry and

   _____ .

2. Dave became angry when he _____ that Joe was flirting with

   Susan.

3. Susan _____ Dave's _____ when she left the party

   with Joe.

4. Joe _____ Susan all night. He said, "You're beautiful! You're

   wonderful! You're an excellent dancer!"

5. Men and women meet in different ways. Sometimes a friend or parent

   introduces them, but sometimes they meet _____ .

6. From the moment Joe noticed Susan, he didn't look at anyone else. He

   _____ Susan all night.

7. The day after the party Susan said to Dave, "Don't worry. You will

   _____ another woman soon."

8. Dave was very angry with Susan and Joe, but he didn't say anything. He

   _____ them all night.

Discussion and Writing

1. Do you know any couples who met in unusual ways? Tell about the time they met.

2. In life, many important things happen by chance or by accident. Tell about a chance event that changed your life, or the life of someone you know.
3. Tell the story in the cartoon.

2. Giving Gifts

The Marvelous Toy

Grammar Focus   Past tense (regular and irregular)

Song Introduction   Did you ever receive a special gift when you were a child? This song by Tom Paxton tells about an unusual gift that a father gave his son. Try to imagine it.

Listening Comprehension   Listen to the song and decide if the following statements are TRUE or NOT TRUE.

1. _____   At first, the son didn't like the toy.

2. _____   The toy didn't make any noise.

3. _____   When the boy became a father, he gave the marvelous toy to *his* son.

9

Song Task   Listen to the song. Fill in the blanks with the past form of the base verb in parentheses.

*The Marvelous Toy**

by Tom Paxton

1   When I (be) _____ just *a wee little lad*   (Scottish dialect) a very little boy

2   Full of health and joy,

3   My father *homeward (come)* _____   came home
      one night.

4   And (give) _____ to me a toy.

5   A wonder *to behold* it (be) _____ .   to look at

6   With many colors bright,

7   And the moment *I (lay)* _____ *eyes on it*   I saw it

9   It (become) _____ my heart's delight.

CHORUS:

9   *It (go)* _____ *"zip"* when it   It made the sound "zip"
      (move) _____

10 And "bop" when it (stop) _____

11 "Wrrrr" when it (stand) _____ still,

12 I never (know) _____ just what it
      (be) _____ ,

13 And I guess I never will.

14 The first time that I (pick) _____ it up,

15 I (have) _____ a big surprise.

16 *'Cause* right on the bottom (be) _____   because
      two big buttons

17 That (look) _____ like big green eyes.

18 I first (push) _____ one and then the
      other,

19 Then I (twist) _____ its *lid,*   top (usually of a jar)

20 And when I *(set)* _____ *it down* again,   put it down

21 Here is what it (do) _____ .

CHORUS

*THE MARVELOUS TOY by Tom Paxton. © Copyright 1964, 1977 Cherry Lane Music Publishing Co., Inc. All rights reserved. Used by permission.

22 The years have gone by too quickly it seems,

23 I have my own little boy,

24 And yesterday I (give) _____ to him
    my marvelous little toy.

25 His eyes nearly (pop) _____ right out
    of his head,

26 And *he (give)* _____ *a squeal of glee*   he shouted with happiness

27 Neither one of us knows just what it is

28 But he loves it just like me.

CHORUS:

29 It still goes "zip" when it moves,

30 And "bop" when it stops,

31 "Wrrrr" when it stands stlll.

32 I never (know) _____ just what it
    (be) _____ ,

33 And I guess I never will.

Grammar Function

We use the simple past tense to talk about completed (finished) actions in
the past.

For example:

Single Action   *Repeated Action*
My father gave me a marvelous toy 30 years   I played with it every day.
ago.

See also *Understanding the Structures,* p. 80.

Structured Practice 1   Here is a summary of the story in the song. The sentences are NOT in the correct order. You must do two things:

a)   Change the base form verbs in parentheses to the past tense.

b)   Put the sentences in the correct order so that the story makes sense. Number the sentences 1–11. The first one is done for you.

_____ I (open) _____ it quickly and (see) _____ my unusual gift.

_____ I (negative/want) _____ to go to bed.

_____ Finally, at 5:30 p.m. he (arrive) _____ .

___1___ It (be) ___*was*___ the evening of my 5th birthday.

_____ He (hand) _____ it to me and (say) _____ , "Happy Birthday!"

_____ It (remain) _____ my favorite gift throughout my life.

_____ He (have) _____ a large box under his arm.

_____ I (love) _____ it as soon as I (see) _____ it.

_____ In the years after that birthday, I often (play) _____ with my marvelous toy.

_____ I (wait) _____ anxiously for my father to come home with my birthday present.

_____ I (watch) _____ it and (play) _____ with it for hours.

Structured Practice 2   *An Unusual Gift*   Here is a small part of a conversation between two people. Use your imagination to decide who A and B are. Who is "he"? What was the occasion? What was the gift? Discuss these questions with a partner. Then add several lines to the beginning and end of the dialog. Use the past tense wherever possible. Practice the dialog with your partner.

A: _____

B: _____

A: He gave you what?!

B: You heard me.

A: That's incredible!

B: I know. I opened my eyes, and when I saw it I almost fainted.

A: Then what did you do?

B: _____

A: _____

B: _____

A: _____

B: _____

Vocabulary   Here are some words that may be useful in your discussion and writing.

a surprise—(noun) something not expected
to surprise someone—(verb) to do something unexpected; (adjective) surprised
excited—(adjective) feeling very happy and eager
disappointed—(adjective) feeling that someone or something did not fulfill your hopes
unique—(adjective) one of a kind
handmade—(adjective) made by hand, not machine
gift—(noun) present
great—(adjective) marvelous, wonderful

Vocabulary Exercise   In the sentences below, fill in the blanks with the correct word or expression from the list above. (You may have to change the form—singular to plural, for example.)

1. The boy in the song felt very _____ when his father gave him the marvelous toy.

2. A _____ sweater is usually more expensive than a machine-made one.

3. My parents refused to show me my birthday present before my birthday. They wanted it to be a complete _____ .

4. I really hoped to see you. I was _____ that you couldn't come to my party.

5. Sometimes I like _____ friends by giving them gifts for no special reason.

6. The birthday present you gave me is _____ ! I absolutely love it! Thanks!

7. It's nice to bring a _____ to friends when they move to a new apartment or house.

8. The marvelous toy is _____ . There is no other toy like it in the world.

Discussion and Writing

1. Do you remember giving or receiving any special gifts when you were a child? In what way were they special?
2. What was the best give you ever gave? What was the best gift you ever received? What was the worst gift you ever gave? What was the worst gift you ever received?
3. Some people say, "It's better to give than to receive." What do you think? Why?

3. Summertime

UNDER THE BOARDWALK

Grammar Focus   Prepositions of place

Song Introduction   Where do you go on a hot summer day? To the beach, of course! Take some friends to talk to, a blanket to sit on, and find a nice place on the beach. Remember—when it gets too hot, you can sit under the boardwalk to get out of the sun. Here is an old rock n' roll song about a popular summer activity.

Listening Comprehension   Listen to the song and decide if the following statements are TRUE or NOT TRUE.

1. _____ It's cool and comfortable to sit under the boardwalk.

2. _____ The singer will sit on his blanket alone.

3. _____ They sell hot dogs and french fries in the park near the beach.

17

Song Task   As you listen to the song, circle the prepositions of place that you hear.

*Under the Boardwalk**
by Artie Resnick and Kenny Young

1   When the *sun beats down* and burns the *tar* up   sun shines brightly / black
    (in/at/on) the roof,   substance you make roads with

2   And your shoes get so hot you wish your tired feet   cannot burn
    were *fireproof,*

3   (Under/Near/Above) the *boardwalk,* down (in/by/   wooden, elevated path near a beach
    across from) the sea,

4   (In/Under/On) a blanket with my baby,

5   That's where I'll be.

CHORUS:

6   (Next to/Under/By) the boardwalk,

7   *Out of the sun,*   not in the sunshine

8   (In/Above/Under) the boardwalk,

9   We'll be having some fun.

10 (Near/Under/On) the boardwalk,

11 People walking (under/by/above),

12 (At/Under/On) the boardwalk,

13 We'll be falling in love,

14 (Across from/In/Under) the boardwalk, board-
    walk.

15 (In/At/From) the park you hear the happy sounds
    of the carousel,

16 You can almost taste the *hot dogs* and *french fries*   frankfurters / french fried potatoes
    they sell.

17 (Under/Above/In) the boardwalk, down (next to/
    between/by) the sea,

18 (Under/On/At) a blanket with my baby,

19 That's where I'll be.

CHORUS

20 (Under/Above/In) the boardwalk, down (next to/
    between/by) the sea,

21 (Under/On/At) a blanket with my baby,

22 That's where I'll be.

CHORUS

Grammar Function

Prepositions are used for different purposes. In this chapter, we are looking at prepositions of place—prepositions which describe the location of people or objects.

For example: He's lying on a blanket under the boardwalk near the park. (See p. 83.)

See also *Understanding the Structures,* p. 82.

Structured Practice 1　Here is a page from a travel guide book on good places to go in the summer. Fill in the missing prepositions. Look at the map and choose from the following prepositions: in, on, at, between, by, near, next to, across from, opposite, under, above.

Welcome to Atlantic Beach! Come and relax _____ our beautiful town _____ the water. Talk a walk _____ the boardwalk, and then cool off _____ the beautiful, blue ocean. The sun always shines_____ you. If it gets too hot, put your blanket _____ the shade _____ the boardwalk.

Stay overnight _____ the new Seaside Hotel _____ the end of the boardwalk, or _____ the Sunshine Motel, which is also _____ the beach.

Spend the day with your children_____ our wonderful amusement park. It's _____ the boardwalk, _____ 7th Street and 9th Street.

In the evening, see a movie _____ our air-conditioned movie theater, _____ Beach Avenue, between 6th and 7th Streets. After the movie, take a long walk _____ the park, which is _____ the movie theater. Have dinner _____ our famous seafood restaurant _____ Shore Road, _____ the Seaside Hotel.

Come and enjoy our beautiful town _____ the beach!

Structured Practice 2   In the first box, draw a picture of your ideal beach. What does it look like? Does it have a boardwalk? Are there many people on it? What are they doing? Are there any trees? buildings? restaurants? Don't show your picture to anyone!

My Ideal Beach

Now, describe your picture to your partner as completely as possible. Remember—don't show the picture to him or her! Your partner will draw your beach in his/her second box, according to your description. Then, your partner will describe his/her beach to you. Draw it in the box below. When you are all finished, compare your pictures and discuss any differences between them.

My Partner's Ideal Beach

Vocabulary   Here are some words that may be useful in your discussion and writing.

suntan—(noun) the brown color fair skin turns after being in the sun
sunburn—(noun) the red and sore skin fair people have after too much time in the sun
to cool off—(verb) to feel cool and refreshed
bathing suit—(noun) clothing people wear for swimming; swimsuit
towel—(noun) a soft cloth a person uses to dry off with
lifeguard—(noun) a person who watches swimmers and protects them from danger
shade—(noun) an area out of direct sunlight
to wade—(verb) to walk through water, usually below the knees

Vocabulary Exercise   In the sentences below, fill in the blanks with the correct word or expression from the list above. (You may have to change the form—singular to plural, for example.)

1. A two-piece _____ is called a bikini.

2. When you sit in the sun too long and your skin turns red and hurts, you have a

   _____ .

3. If you want to get a little wet but don't want to swim, you can_____

   in the water.

4. To be a good _____ you have to be a very strong swimmer.

5. After sitting in the sun, you can _____ by swimming or having a

   cool drink.

6. It's good to have a large _____ to lie on at the beach.

7. When you lie in the sun and your skin turns brown, you have a_____ .

8. On a hot day at the beach, it isn't good to sit in the sun for a long time. It's good

   to sit in the _____ under the boardwalk or under a tree.

Discussion and Writing

1. Where do people go to "cool off" on a hot, summer day in your country? Describe this place.
2. Think about the hottest day you can remember. Where were you? How hot was it? When was it? What did you do?
3. Write a page for a travel brochure describing your favorite beach town or vacation spot. Try to convince people that this is the best place to spend a vacation.

4. Good Days, Bad Days

Oh, What a Beautiful Mornin'

Grammar Focus   Present continuous tense

Song Introduction   *Oh, What a Beautiful Mornin'* comes from the musical, *Oklahoma*. It is one of Broadway's most famous songs. In it, the singer describes the beautiful morning scene that he is looking at.

Listening Comprehension   Listen to the song and decide if the following statements are TRUE or NOT TRUE.

1. _____   The singer is in the city.

2. _____   It's raining outside.

3. _____   The singer is very happy.

Song Task   Look at the pictures. As you listen to the song, find the sentence from the song that describes the picture. Write the number of the line near the picture.

Oh, What a Beautiful Mornin'*
by Richard Rodgers and Oscar Hammerstein, II

1   (Well,) There's a bright, *golden haze* on the meadow,   sunshine
2   There's a bright golden haze on the meadow.
3   The corn is as high as an elephant's eye,
4   And it looks like it's climbing clear up to the sky.

CHORUS:
5   (Well,) Oh, what a beautiful *mornin'*,   morning
6   Oh, what a beautiful day.
7   I've got a beautiful feeling,
8   Everything's going my way.

9   All the cattle are standing like statues,
10   All the cattle are standing like statues,
11   They don't turn their heads as they see me ride by,
12   But a little, brown *maverick* is winking her eye. (She says...)   young cow or horse

CHORUS:
13   Oh, what a beautiful mornin', (yeah)
14   Oh, what a beautiful day. (I want you all to know ...)
15   I've got a beautiful feeling,
16   Everything's going my way. (yeah)

17   All the sounds of the earth are like music,
18   All the sounds of the earth are like music.
19   The breeze is so busy *it don't miss a tree,*   there is a strong breeze
20   And an old, weeping willow is laughing at me. (She said...)

CHORUS:
21   Oh, what a beautiful mornin', (yeah, yeah)
22   Oh, what a beautiful day.
23   I've got a beautiful feeling,
24   Everything's going my way.
25   Oh, what a beautiful day.

*OH, WHAT A BEAUTIFUL MORNIN'. Copyright © 1943 by Richard Rodgers and Oscar Hammerstein, II. Copyright renewed Williamson Music Inc., Owner of publication and allied rights for the Western Hemisphere and Japan (administered by Chappell & Co., Inc.). International Copyright Secured. ALL RIGHTS RESERVED. Used by permission.

Grammar Function

One of the functions of the present continuous tense is to describe actions that are happening exactly at this moment.

For example: Right now, the sun is shining.

For this function, we use phrases like *now* and *at this moment.*

We also use the present continuous tense to talk about the present in a more general way.

For example: Everything is going well at work. (maybe not at this *exact* moment, but *now*—this month or this week)

For this function, we use phrases like *today, these days, nowadays, this (week/month/year), this semester.*

See also *Understanding the Structures,* p. 84.

Structured Practice 1   Howie and Mark are truck drivers who are very different. They are on their way to Chicago to make a delivery. In the conversation below, fill in the blanks with the present continuous tense of the verbs in parentheses.

Howie: Hey, slow down! You (speed) _____ !

Mark: No, I'm not. I (go) _____ 55 miles per hour. I (drive) _____ now. Don't worry about it. You know I'm a good driver. What (bother) _____ you?

Howie: I'm very uncomfortable. It's very hot in here.

Mark: Look on the bright side. It's a beautiful morning. The sun (shine) _____ and we (drive) _____ through a beautiful part of the country.

Howie: Yes, but the air conditioner (negative/work) _____ and I (die) _____ of the heat.

Mark: Let's change the subject. How (do) _____ the Yankees _____ ?

Howie: Terribly! They (play) _____ much worse than last season. They (negative/win) _____ many games.

Mark: Okay. Let's not talk about sports. How about the economy? I'm sure you're not pessimistic about that.

Howie: Well, I'm not optimistic about it. I (make) _____ more money now than last year, but I (spend) _____ more also. Prices (rise) _____ in everything.

Mark: You're too negative! Things (improve) _____ slowly. You (negative/try) _____ to see the good side.

Howie: I guess we see things differently.

Structured Practice 2 People often see things differently. Look at the picture and decide what you see happening and why. For example, do you think the person is happy or sad? What is he feeling? What is he thinking about? Write your description; then share it with a partner.

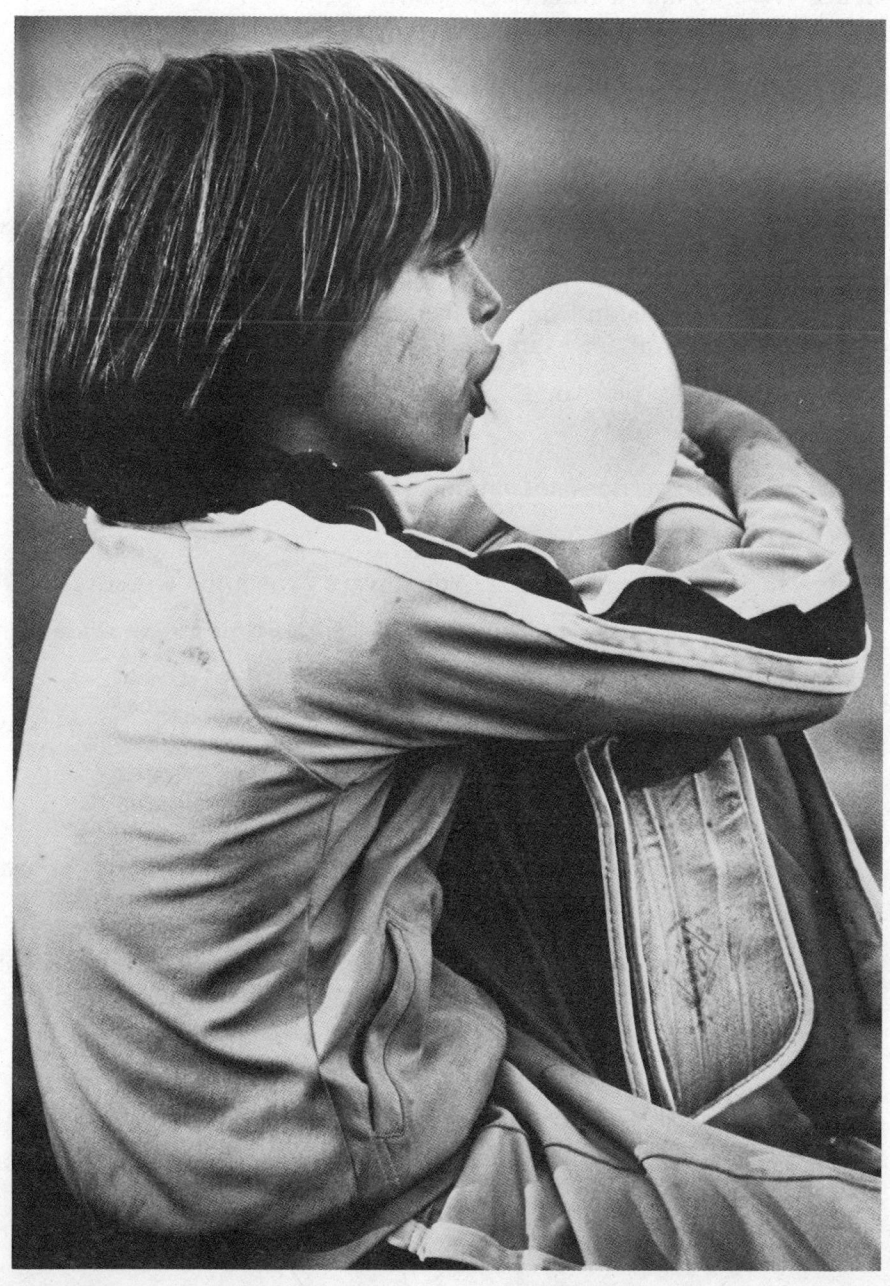

Vocabulary   Here are some words that may be useful in your discussion and writing.

optimist—(noun) a person who looks at the good points of a situation
pessimist—(noun) a person who looks at the bad points of a situation
to stroll—(verb) to take a walk for pleasure
to jog—(verb) to run at a moderate speed
to rush—(verb) to hurry; move quickly
to look on the bright side—(idiom) to emphasize the good part of a situation
   instead of the bad
gradual—(adjective) slow; little by little
drastic—(adjective) severe; sudden and sharp

Vocabulary Exercise   In the sentences below, fill in the blanks with the correct word or expression from the list above. (You may have to change the form—singular to plural, for example.)

1. On a sunny day, it's pleasant _____ through a park and enjoy the
   beautiful day.

2. Making new friends does not happen quickly. It is usually a _____
   process that takes time.

3. You're such a _____ . You always expect the worst results.

4. I always wake up early and give myself a lot of time to get ready in the
   morning because I hate _____ .

5. Yesterday it was 80°F and sunny; today it's 50°F and rainy. That's a very
   _____ change in the weather!

6. I'm an _____ . I always expect things to work out well.

7. Erica loves to exercise. She _____ three miles every morning
   before she goes to work.

8. My father was a real optimist. Whenever I felt sad or upset about something,
   he taught me _____ .

Discussion and Writing

1. Look out the nearest window and take notes. Write down everything that is happening for three or four minutes. Pay attention to people, cars, sounds, the weather, etc. Now discuss what you saw with a partner. Did he/she see the same things? What was different?
2. Tell about some important changes or events that are taking place in your life right now (this week, month, semester, or year).
3. Are you an optimist or a pessimist? Why do you consider yourself that way? Give some examples.

5. Following the Crowd

LITTLE BOXES

Grammar Focus   Simple present tense

Song Introduction   Society has strong rules of behavior. Some people follow society's rules completely: they never ask "why?" They always "follow the crowd." The song *Little Boxes* is about these people.

Listening Comprehension   Listen to the song and decide if the following statements are TRUE or NOT TRUE.

1. _____ All the houses are different colors, but they look the same.

2. _____ The people think it's good to be different.

3. _____ The children follow their parents' lifestyle.

Song Task Listen to the song. Use what you hear *and* your knowledge of English to fill in the missing words. (Write only one word per line.)

Little Boxes*
by Malvina Reynolds

1 Little boxes on the hillside
2 Little boxes *made of ticky tacky*
3 Little boxes, little boxes
4 Little boxes all the same.
5 _____ a green one and a pink one
6 And a blue one and a yellow one,
7 And they're all made out of ticky tacky
8 And _____ all look just the same.

9 And the _____ in the houses
10 All _____ to the university
11 And they all get put in boxes,
12 Little boxes all the same.
13 And there's doctors and there's lawyers
14 And business executives
15 And they're all made out of ticky tacky
16 And they all _____ just the same.

17 And they all _____ on the golf course
18 And _____ their martini dry
19 And _____ all have pretty children
20 And the _____ go to school.
21 And the children _____ to summer camp
22 And then to the university
23 And _____ all get put in boxes
24 And they all _____ out the same.

25 And the _____ go into business
26 And _____ and raise a family
27 And they all get put in boxes
28 Little boxes all the same

not in style or good taste; cheap-looking

*Little Boxes. Words and music by Malvina Reynolds. © 1962 Schroder Music Co. Used by permission. All rights reserved.

29 _____ a green one and a pink one

30 And a blue one and a yellow one

31 And _____ all made out of ticky tacky

32 And they all _____ just the same.

Grammar Function

We use the simple present tense for three main purposes:

to make a generalization—All the boys go into business.

to talk about a routine action—The children go to summer camp every summer.

to talk about a general truth—The houses all look the same.

See also *Understanding the Structures*, p. 86.

Structured Practice 1
Elaine Silver and Richard Korman got married in July, 1982. They are different from traditional couples in many ways. In this interview, Elaine and Richard discuss their marriage and their beliefs. Fill in the blanks with the simple present tense of the verb in parentheses.

Interviewer: I know that you both (work) _____ . What _____ you (do) _____ ?

Elaine: I (work) _____ for a large publishing company. . . .

Richard: . . . and I'm an artist.

I: I see. And how _____ you (divide) _____ your household responsibilities?

E: We (divide) _____ all the work equally. For example, one week I (cook) _____ dinner and Richard (wash) _____ the dishes, and one week I (wash) _____ and he (cook) _____ .

R: I (paint) _____ at home so sometimes I (do) _____ some extra work in the house. I (negative/mind) _____ .

I: Some men (negative/feel) _____ comfortable about working in the house. They (say) _____ it's "women's work."

R: Well, I completely (disagree) _____ . These men (feel)

_____ superior to women. I (believe) _____ that men

and women are completely equal.

I: Elaine, _____ you (use) _____ your husband's family

name?

E: No, I (negative/belong) _____ to my husband. Why

_____ I (need) _____ his name? I (have)

_____ my own name.

I: I (know) _____ that Richard (accept) _____ that, but

_____ your parents (understand) _____ your

feelings?

E: Not really. They are very traditional. My father (write) _____

"Mrs. Richard Korman" on letters and I always (get) _____ angry!

He (negative/accept) _____ my decision to keep my own name.

My mother (respect) _____ my decision, but she (negative/

believe) _____ it's important.

Structured Practice 2   With a partner, take turns asking and answering
the following questions:

1. Do Elaine and Richard think that following the rules of society is important?
2. Do you agree with Elaine's decision to keep her name? Why or why not?
3. Why does Elaine's father address letters to Mrs. Richard Korman?
4. Does Richard think names are important?
5. How does Richard feel about housework?
6. Do married women in your country work?
7. In your country, do some women earn more money than their husbands?
8. Do married women in your country take their husbands' names?
9. Do men in your country help with the housework?
10. How do young couples in your country feel about marriage?

Vocabulary Here are some words that may be useful in your discussion and writing.

a nonconformist—(noun) a person who doesn't act or think according to society's rules and values
to follow the crowd—(idiom) to think and do what most people do
traditional—(adjective) following rules, customs, or beliefs of society
old-fashioned—(adjective) not modern
a housewife—(noun) a married woman who takes care of her house and family, but does not earn a salary (plural—housewives)
to work outside the home—(idiom) to have a job with a salary
to support a family—(idiom) to provide money for a family's needs
independent—(adjective) thinking for yourself and acting according to your own ideas

Vocabulary Exercise In the sentences below, fill in the blanks with the correct word or expression from the list above. (You may have to change the form—singular to plural, for example.)

1. _____ do not earn a salary, but they work very hard at home.

2. In many cultures, it is more important to _____ than to be different from others.

3. Elaine and Richard are _____ because they don't follow society's "rules" about marriage.

4. Today, it is very common for men and women to _____ in order to make enough money to live on.

5. _____ people like to make their own decisions—sometimes they keep traditions, and sometimes they don't.

6. In the United States, it is a _____ custom for married women to use their husbands' family name.

7. In the old days, it was only the man's responsibility to _____ .

8. Elaine and Richard think that some traditional customs are _____ and not necessary in the modern world.

Discussion and Writing

1. What do the little boxes in the song represent?
2. Of course each person's life is different, but there are many generalizations that we can make about typical lifestyles in various countries. For example, in the United States most people set up their own home after they finish university, even if they are not married. What are some of the "rules of society" that people in your country follow? Write them in the "little boxes" below. In my country. . . .

Example:

Children live with
their parents until
they get married.

3. Is it easy to be a nonconformist in your country? Do you know anyone who is a nonconformist? Describe that person.
4. Write another stanza to the song about a particular lifestyle or group of people in your country (e.g., women, teenagers, workers, old people, etc.). Try to follow the rhythm of the song.

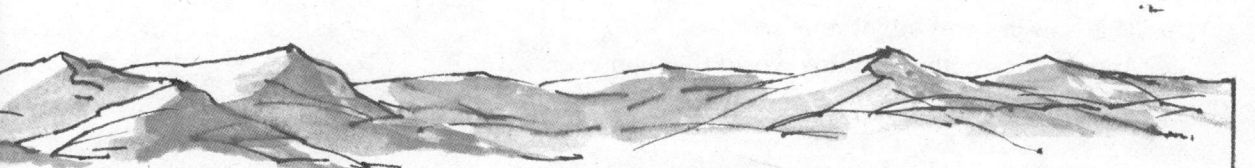

6. Stretching the Truth

My Love

Grammar Focus   Comparative and superlative forms of adjectives (-er and more; -est and most)

Song Introduction   In *My Love* the singer compares her love to many things. Because she is so excited about her love, she exaggerates her comparisons. In other words, she says things that are unbelievable. She isn't really lying, but she *is* "stretching the truth."

Listening Comprehension   Listen to the song and decide if the following statements are TRUE or NOT TRUE.

1. _____   The singer compares her love to the sky.

2. _____   The singer is very deeply in love.

3. _____   A sigh is a soft sound.

Song Task   Listen to the song. Use what you hear *and* your knowledge of English to fill in the missing words. (Write only one word per line.)

*My Love**
by Tony Hatch

CHORUS:

1   My love is _____ than the warmest
      sunshine,

2   Softer _____ a sigh,

3   My love is deeper than _____ _____
      ocean,

4   _____ than the sky.

5   My love is _____ than the _____
      star

6   That shines every night above,

7   And there is nothing in this world that can ever
      change _____ love.

8   Something happened _____ my heart

9   The day that I met you,

10 Something that I never felt _____ .

11 *You are _____ on my mind,*   I'm always thinking about you.

12 No matter what I do,

13 And every day it seems I want you_____ .

CHORUS

14 Once I thought that love was meant

15 For anyone else but _____ ,

16 *Once I thought you'd never come my way.*   Once I thought I would never meet
                                                    someone like you. / It demonstrates

17 Now it *only goes to show*

18 How wrong we _____ can be,

19 For now I have to tell you every_____ .

CHORUS

*"MY LOVE." Words and music by Tony Hatch. © copyright 1965 by Welbeck Music, Ltd. London, England. Sole selling agent, Duchess Music Corporation (MCA), New York, N.Y. for USA and Canada. Used by permission. All rights reserved.

Grammar Function

We use the comparative form of adjectives to describe differences between two things.

For example:

Learning a second language as an adult is $\left\{ \begin{array}{l} \text{harder} \\ \text{more difficult} \end{array} \right\}$ than learning a second language as a child.

We use the superlative form to describe a unique characteristic of one thing among many.

For example:

Sometimes I think English is the $\left\{ \begin{array}{l} \text{hardest} \\ \text{most difficult} \end{array} \right\}$ language to learn.

See also *Understanding the Structures*, p. 88.

Structured Practice 1   James wants to buy a new car. He is now at George's Gorgeous Used Car Lot. James does not have a lot of money, so he doesn't want to make a mistake. He wants a car that is cheap but good. In the dialog below, fill in the blanks with the comparative or superlative form of the adjective in parentheses, as is necessary.

George: Can I help you, sir?

James: I'm looking for a used car. I saw a green Ford over there. It looks nice.

How much is it?

George: Oh, that isn't very good. It is (cheap) _____ car in the lot, so everyone always asks about it. But it's in pretty bad shape.

James: I need a car that will be (sturdy) _____ my last car.

George: I have a couple of cars to show you! This Datsun is only two years old. This Volkswagen is a little bit (old) _____ the Datsun, but it uses very little gas, so it's (economical) _____ the Datsun.

James: How much are they?

George: Don't worry about money! I'll give you a good deal.

James: Yes, but I don't have a lot of money. Is the Volkswagen (cheap) _____ the Datsun?

George: Well, yes, but the Datsun is really perfect for you. It's (fast) _____ car I have, and it's also (new) _____ . It's (comfortable) _____ of all the cars on this lot.

James: How much is it?

George: It's only a little bit (expensive) _____ the Volkswagen. And it's certainly a lot (nice) _____ the Volkswagen.

James: But how much is it?

George: Well, for you, only $9,000.

James: What!! This old Datsun is (expensive) _____ my last car when it was new!

George: Maybe, but this car is probably a lot (good) _____ your old car. As a matter of fact, this car is (good) _____ car I have.

James: Maybe so, but I can't spend that much money. How much is that green Ford that I asked you about before?

George: It's $500.

James: I'll take it.

George: You'll be sorry!

Structured Practice 2   People often exaggerate when they try to sell you something. They compare their product to another one and explain that theirs is better, or stronger, or more economical. Sometimes they compare their product to all the others and tell you that theirs is the best, or the strongest, or the most economical.

Imagine that you work for an advertising agency. With a partner, write a thirty second commercial for a particular product (for example, a hamburger, a brand of toothpaste, an airline, jeans). Make sure you give your product a name. Explain how your product is better than all the other products on the market.

Vocabulary   Here are some words that may be useful in your discussion and writing.

to persuade—(verb) to convince
to brag—(verb) to praise yourself in an exaggerated way
crowded—(adjective) full of people
sturdy—(adjective) built well
to stretch the truth—(idiom) to exaggerate
to last—(verb) to remain in good condition
a lie—(noun) something that is not true
a white lie—(noun) a lie someone tells in order not to hurt another person

Vocabulary Exercise   In the sentences below, fill in the blanks with the correct word or expression from the list above. (You may have to change the form—singular to plural, for example.)

1. Advertisers often _____ about their product in order to make it more attractive to customers.

2. The hostess asked me how I liked the dessert. It was terrible but I didn't want to hurt her feelings. I told a _____ and said that it was delicious.

3. Rush hour is the time when most people travel to and from work. During rush hour the trains, buses, and streets are always more _____ than at other times.

4. Used car salesmen usually try _____ their customers to buy the most expensive car on their lot.

5. The divorce rate is much higher today than it was in the past. Nowadays, many marriages only _____ a few years.

6. Yesterday I was annoyed at Alice because she _____ about her new apartment. She said, "My apartment has the best view in the city, and it is roomier than your apartment, and certainly cheaper."

7. You have to be careful when you buy a used car. The salesmen often tell _____ about the car's age and quality.

8. These shoes are not very _____ . I bought them last month and they are already falling apart.

Discussion and Writing

1. What is the difference between a lie, a white lie, and an exaggeration? Give examples of each.
2. What are some common things that people exaggerate? Why do you think they exaggerate?
3. What are some unique characteristics of your native country or city? For example, Tokyo is *the most populated* city in the world. Try to write about five characteristics.
4. Imagine that you received a letter from a foreign friend. The friend is planning to live in your country for one year but cannot decide where to live. Write a letter to your friend. In the letter, compare your city with other cities and areas in your country. Discuss the advantages and disadvantages of each.

UNITED STATES POSTAGE 1¢

7. Letters

I'm gonna sit right down and write myself a letter

Grammar Focus   Future tense

Song Introduction   Fats Waller was a black jazz musician. *I'm Gonna Sit Right Down and Write Myself a Letter* is a song that he made popular. In this song, a man writes a letter to *himself* and pretends it is from the woman he loves.

Listening Comprehension   Listen to the song and decide if the following statements are TRUE or NOT TRUE.

1. _____ The singer is going to write a letter to his girlfriend.

2. _____ The letter will be a "love-letter."

3. _____ The singer will feel wonderful when he reads the letter.

Song Task   Underline the verbs that tell about actions in the future. The first two are done for you.

Note: When a sentence tells about two actions completed by one subject and connected by AND, don't repeat the subject and helping verb.

Example: I'm going to sit right down and write myself a letter.

I'm Gonna Sit Right Down and Write Myself a Letter***
by F. Ahlert and J. Young

1   I'm *gonna sit right down* and write myself a letter (yes, yes)   I'm going to sit down immediately

2   And *make believe* it came from you (you, I love you, love you)   pretend

3   I'm gonna write words oh so sweet,

4   *They're gonna knock me off* these (size 12) *feet,*   They're going to completely surprise me

5   A lot of kisses on the bottom (kisses on the bottom, yes)

6   I'll be glad I got 'em.

7   I'm gonna smile and say "Gee, I hope you're feeling better."

8   (Better, better, it's a killer)

9   And *close "with love"* the way you do, (you do.)   end the letter with the words "with love"

10   I'm gonna sit right down and write myself a postcard,

11   (*I gotta save some money,* you know, yes)   I have to save some money

12   And make believe, make believe,

13   I'm gonna make believe it came from you.

---

*Note: When *going to* means *will* and it comes before another verb (example: I'm going to sit down), we say "gonna." DON'T write *gonna*—just say it that way. It is always written in the full form—*going to*—except in some songs and advertisements.

Grammar Function

The future tense (will/going to) has four main purposes. They are:

to make a promise or express willingness—I'll write to you. *I won't* forget!

*to make a prediction—*Don't worry. I'm sure *he'll write* to you. *He won't forget.*

to state a plan or intention—I'm going to write a letter to my brother. *I'm not going to call* him.

For *general future actions* that are not clearly promises, predictions, or plans, you can use *will* OR *going to.*

See also *Understanding the Structures,* p. 89.

Structured Practice 1

In the song the singer describes an unusual plan. He is going to write a beautiful love-letter to himself! Why? Well, look at the letter he received from his girlfriend yesterday. Fill in the blanks with the future tense form of the verb in parentheses. Information that will help you choose between *will* and *going to* is written below the lines.

Dear John,

I know that you (be) _____ surprised to receive a letter like this
                              PREDICTION
from me. I (tell)_____ you something that is not easy to say. Please try
                 INTENTION
to understand. I met a man who asked me to marry him and I (accept)

_____ his offer.
   INTENTION
I know that we made an agreement many years ago. I remember your exact

words: "I'm not ready to get married now but I (marry) _____ you
                                                        GENERAL FUTURE
some day. I (be) _____ a good husband to you." I remember my
                 PROMISE
answer to you: "I (wait) _____ until you are ready to marry me." I
                          PROMISE
waited and waited. Then I met Patrick. He asked me the question that you

(negative/ask)_____ ever _____ : "(marry)
                           PREDICTION
_____ you _____ me?" I waited 10 years to hear those
        WILLINGNESS
four little words from you. Now I realize that you (ask)

_____ never _____ that question.
              INTENTION
I know what you (say) _____ . Another man (negative/love)
                        PREDICTION
_____ me as much as you do. Maybe that's true. You (be)
 PREDICTION

_____ always _____ in my thoughts and I (forget)
                    PREDICTION
_____ never _____ you, but I (marry) _____
         PROMISE   INTENTION
someone else. I'm sorry, John.

Love,

Karen

Structured Practice 2   Sit down and write a letter—not to yourself!—but to a friend. In the letter tell your friend about some plans you have for your next vacation. Ask your friend what his/her plans are and invite your friend to join you. Be as specific about your plans as you can. We have begun the letter for you.

Dear Charlie,

How are you? I'm sorry I haven't written for a long time but I've been very busy making plans for my vacation. I'm very excited. I'm sure I will have a fantastic time. This is what I plan to do: _____

_____

_____

Take care,

Vocabulary   Here are some words that may be useful in your discussion and writing.

to make plans—(verb) to make arrangements for a future activity
to predict—(verb) to describe a future event before it happens
intention—(noun) a decision to act in a certain way (often used as a negative: I have no intention of (verb)ing)
by myself—alone, with no help from others
to mail—(verb) to send a letter or package (British English = to post)
to improve—(verb) to make or get better
New Year's resolution—(noun) a decision made on New Year's Day to do or stop doing something in the coming year
to break a promise—(idiom) to *not* do something that you promised to do

Vocabulary Exercise   In the sentences below, fill in the blanks with the correct word or expression from the list above. (You may have to change the form—singular to plural, for example.)

1. "I stopped smoking on January 1st. It was my most important

   _____."

2. Before going on a vacation, it's a good idea to go to a travel agency. The travel

   agent can help you _____.

3. "I _____ a postcard to you when I was on vacation. Did you

   receive it?"

4. Pollution is a very serious problem in many cities. Many people hope that

   their governments will do something about it, and that the situation will

   _____.

5. Karen promised John to wait for him and marry him. But in her letter, she

   _____ her _____.

6. Astrology, the study of the stars, is an ancient way _____ the

   future. Today, many people still believe in it.

7. I don't like to study with other people. I prefer to study _____.

8. I plan to study English until I speak it fluently. I have no _____ of

   leaving school before then.

Discussion and Writing

1. New Year's Eve, December 31st, is a time when people think about the past and discuss the changes that will occur in the new year. They make resolutions (promises) to themselves about ways they will change, and they make predictions about what will happen in the world. Imagine that it is New Year's Eve. With your partner, talk about the following:
   a. personal plans (work, studies, travel, etc.)
   b. personal promises (What will you do to improve or change your life?)
   c. changes in your country (political, social, economic)
2. Did you ever receive an important letter or a letter that changed your life in any way? Tell about it.
3. Imagine that you are a famous person (politician, musician, actor, scientist, criminal, etc.). Write a letter telling a friend about your plans for the coming year. Tell about any New Year's resolutions that you made.

8. A Fresh Start

TIE A YELLOW RIBBON 'ROUND THE OLD OAK TREE

Grammar Focus   Real conditional

Song Introduction   The song *Tie a Yellow Ribbon 'Round the Old Oak Tree* is based on a true story. A man named Vingo spent three years in jail. Before he left prison, he wrote a letter to his wife. He wrote, "If you still love me, tie a yellow ribbon around the tree near our house. If I don't see a yellow ribbon, I will stay on the bus and I will try to forget you."

Listening Comprehension   Listen to the song and decide if the following statements are TRUE or NOT TRUE.

1. _____ The singer is out of jail.

2. _____ If his wife loves him, she will wear a yellow ribbon in her hair.

3. _____ The wife doesn't want her husband to return.

53

Song Task Listen to the song. Use what you hear *and* your knowledge of English to fill in the missing words. (Write only one word per line.)

*Tie a Yellow Ribbon 'Round the Old Oak Tree**
by L. Russell Brown

1 I'm coming _____ , *I've done my time.* I've been in jail.
2 Now, *I've got to know* what is and isn't mine. I have to know.
3 If you received my _____
4 Telling you I'd soon be free,
5 Then you'll know just what to do
6 If you still _____ me,
7 If you still want me.

CHORUS:

8 Oh, tie a yellow ribbon *'round* the old oak tree. around
9 It's been three long _____ .
10 Do you still want me? (still want me)
11 If I _____ see a ribbon 'round the old
      oak tree,
12 I'll _____ on the bus, forget about us,
13 *Put the blame on me,* Say that I'm responsible
14 If I don't see a yellow ribbon 'round the old oak
      tree.

15 Bus _____ , please look for me.
16 *'Cause I couldn't bear* to see what I might see. because I am very afraid
17 I'm really still in _____ ,
18 And my love, she holds the key.
19 A simple, yellow _____ 's
20 What I need *to set me free,* to free me
21 I wrote and told her, "Please . . ."

CHORUS:

22 Oh, tie a yellow ribbon 'round the old oak tree.
23 It's been three long _____ .
24 Do you still want me?

25 If I _____ see a ribbon 'round the old
      oak tree,
26 I'll _____ on the bus, forget about us,
27 Put the blame on me,
28 If I don't see a yellow ribbon 'round the old oak
      tree.

29 Now, the whole damn bus is cheering
30 And I can't believe I _____
31 A hundred yellow ribbons 'round the old oak tree!
      (I'm coming home, um hum.
      Tie a ribbon . . .)

Grammar Function

Like the future tense, the main function of the real conditional is to tell about a plan or intention for the future. But in this case, the future plan depends on something else.

For example:

Future Tense
Vingo will get off the bus.

Real Conditional
If he sees a yellow ribbon, Vingo will get off the bus.

See also *Understanding the Structures*, p. 90.

Structured Practice 1   Before Vingo left prison, he talked with his cellmate (roommate in prison), Harry, about his hopes and fears about the future. In the conversation below, fill in the blanks with the correct form of the verbs in parentheses. You will also have to fill in *can*, *may*, and *will* in the result clause.

Harry: Vingo, you're going home in three days.

Vingo: I'm not so sure. If my wife _____ me anymore, I
              (negative/love)
   _____ _____ home again.
      (neg. modal)   (go)

Harry: I'm sure she loves you.

Vingo: But how will I know?

Harry: You have to find out how she feels. It _____ _____
                   (neg. modal)   (be)
   a surprise if you _____ before you get home.
                (find out)

Vingo: How can I do that? She never writes or calls me.

Harry: Write her a letter and tell her that you want to come home. If she
   _____ you, she _____ _____ you.
       (want)   (modal)   (tell)

Vingo: But I'm leaving in three days! If I _____ it today, she
                            (send)
   _____ _____ my letter in two days. But she
      (modal)   (receive)
   won't have time to answer.

Harry: I have an idea! Isn't there a big tree in front of your house?

Vingo: Yes, an old oak tree.

Harry: In your letter, tell your wife to tie a ribbon around the oak tree if she
   _____ you to come home. If she _____ the
      (want)   (tie)
   ribbon around the tree, you _____ _____ that
                         (modal)   (know)
   she loves you.

Vingo: And if I _____ a ribbon on the tree, I _____
           (negative/see)   (neg. modal)
   _____ the bus. If she _____ me, I _____
      (get off)   (negative/want)   (modal)
   _____ to Florida and begin a new life without her.
      (go)

Harry: Okay, but don't worry. I'm sure she will tie the ribbon around the tree.

Structured Practice 2   Vingo is, of course, very happy to be home. But he is also very worried about his future. In the following dialog, he and his wife discuss their feelings. Complete the sentences in their conversation.

Vingo: I'm so happy to be home again. I want to start a new life now.

Randy: I'll help you in any way I can, but you know it may be difficult.

Vingo: I know. I am an ex-con. It may be difficult to find a job.

Randy: Don't worry. If you don't find a job right away, _____

_____ .

Vingo: But if you _____ , who will take

care of the children?

Randy: I will try to find a job in the evening. I have another idea.

Vingo: What?

Randy: If you _____ , you can go back to

school.

Vingo: School! That's a great idea! If I go back to school, _____

_____ .

Randy: Yes, a new profession is a good idea.

Vingo: I want to make a fresh start and forget about my past. But I'm worried.

Randy: Why?

Vingo: If people discover I'm an ex-con, _____

_____ .

Randy: Vingo, listen to me. That's all behind you. You are a good person and a

hard worker. You will succeed if you really _____ .

Vingo: _____

_____

Randy: _____

_____

Vocabulary Here are some words that may be useful in your discussion and writing.

to make a fresh start—(idiom) to make a new beginning
ex-con—(noun) a person who was once in prison
criminal—(noun) a person who committed a crime
jail—(noun) prison
to get out of jail—(verb) to leave jail
that's all behind you—(idiom) that's in your past
nervous—(adjective) anxious and worried
excited—(adjective) eager and happy

Vocabulary Exercise In the sentences below, fill in the blanks with the correct word or expression from the list above. (You may have to change the form—singular to plural, for example.)

1. Employers often will not hire a person who was once a criminal. Therefore, _____ frequently have trouble finding jobs.

2. Before he left prison, Vingo felt very _____ because he didn't know if his wife wanted him to come home.

3. Vingo spent three years in _____ .

4. When they leave prison, ex-cons hope they can begin their lives again. They want to forget about their past and _____ .

5. Vingo felt very _____ when he saw all the yellow ribbons on the tree.

6. A person who commits a crime is called a _____ .

7. Immediately after he _____ , Vingo took a bus home.

8. Vingo was very worried about finding a job because of his past. His wife said, "Don't worry about your time in jail. _____ ."

Discussion and Writing

1. Discuss the problems of ex-cons in society. Can an ex-con make a "fresh start" in your country?
2. Role play—An employer is looking for a worker who is well trained and very reliable. Two people apply for the job. One is a high school graduate with good references but little experience. The other is an ex-con with excellent work experience. With your assistant, discuss the applicants and decide whom to choose. One person should be the employer and the other his/her assistant.
3. Ex-cons are not the only people who make fresh starts. Many people decide to make new beginnings at different times in their lives. Did you ever decide to make a fresh start? Tell about your decision. Were you successful?
4. Think about some things that may or may not happen to you in the future. For example, if you learn to speak English fluently, how will your life be different? If you win a lot of money, what will you do with it? With a partner, tell at least four things about yourself.

9. Personal Expectations

I'LL KNOW

Grammar Focus   Future time clauses

Song Introduction   *Guys and Dolls* is one of Broadway's most popular musicals. In the play, a very surprising thing happens: a gambler (Sky) and a traditional woman (Sarah) fall in love. Sky and Sarah have very different backgrounds and ideas. In the song *I'll Know,* Sky and Sarah compare their different expectations of love.

Listening Comprehension   Listen to the song and decide if the following statements are TRUE or NOT TRUE.

1. _____   Sarah doesn't know what her love will look like.

2. _____   Sky Masterson thinks that Sarah's expectations are unrealistic.

3. _____   Sky's true love will be a chemist.

61

Song Task   Listen to the song. Circle the correct form of the verb in parentheses. Choose between the simple present and future tenses.

*I'll Know**
by Frank Loesser

Sky: I'm not interested in what he will not be. I'm interested in what he will be.

Sarah: Well, don't worry, I'll know. *For* I've imagined every bit of him, from *his strong moral fiber to the wisdom in his head, to the homey aroma of his pipe.*

Because

all the good qualities he will have

Sky: You have wished yourself *a real dumb character, a square-thinking, pencil-pushing type.*

a very stupid person

a very conservative person

Sarah: Yes, and I *shall* meet him when the time is right.

will (shall = formal or British English; will = American English)

Sky: You've got your guy all figured out, huh?

Sarah: I have.

Sky: Including what he smokes, all figured out.

Sarah: All figured out.

1   I (know/'ll know) when my love (comes/'ll come) along,

2   I won't take a chance.

3   I'll know he'll be just what I need,

4   Not some *fly-by-night* Broadway romance.

temporary

5   *Sky:*   And you'll know *at a glance* by the *crease* in his pants.

immediately / fold

6   *Sarah:*   Yes, I'll know by that calm steady voice.

7   Those feet on the ground.

8   I (know/'ll know) as I (run/'ll run) to his arms

9   That at last I've come home safe and sound.

10   And till then I shall wait,

11   And till then I'll be strong

12   For I (know/'ll know) when my love (comes/'ll come) along.

Sky: No, no, no. You're talking about love. You can't *dope* it like that. What are you picking—a guy or a horse?   explain (gamblers' slang)

Sarah: Oh, I wouldn't expect a gambler to understand.

Sky: Would you like to hear how a gambler feels about the big love deal?

Sarah: No.

Sky: Well, I'll tell you.

Mine will come as a surprise to me.

Mine I leave to *chance and chemistry*.   luck; fate

Sarah: Chemistry?

Sky: Yeah, chemistry.

13 I (know/'ll know) when my love (comes/'ll come)
     along.

14 I'll know then and there.

15 I'll know at the sight of her face,

16 How I care, how I care, how I care.

17 And I'll stop, and I'll stare.

18 And I (know/'ll know) long before we (can speak/
     'll be able to speak)

19 And I'll know in my heart,

20 And I'll know, and I won't ever ask

21 Am I right? *Am I wise? Am I smart?*   Am I intelligent?

22 And I'll stop and I'll stare

23 At that face in the *throng*.   crowd, large group of people

24 Yes, I (know/'ll know) when my love (comes/
     'll come) along.

25 I (know/'ll know) when my love (comes/'ll come)
     along.

Grammar Function

We use future time clauses to talk about future actions in relation to a specific point or time in the future.

For example:

Sarah will get married. (future tense only, no specific time is mentioned)

Sarah will get married *when she meets the right man.* (future tense + future time clause)

Don't let the present tense after the time word confuse you! You are still speaking about the *future.*

See also *Understanding the Structures,* p. 92.

Structured Practice 1   It's the last week of school and three university students are having lunch together in the cafeteria. Fill in the blanks with the simple present tense or the future tense of the verb in parentheses as is necessary.

Steve: _____ you (return) _____ to Venezuela as soon as

school (be) _____ over?

Rosa: No. First I'm going to travel around the U.S. with my brother.

Steve: Where are you going to go?

Rosa: I don't know. As soon as he (arrive) _____ , we (plan)

_____ our trip. After we (spend) _____ a few days

in New York, we (rent) _____ a car and (drive)

_____ west. I (negative/make) _____ any other

plans until he (come) _____ . How about you, Masa?

_____ you (take) _____ a vacation before you (go

back) _____ to Japan?

Masa: No. I have other plans. A few days after I (return) _____ to

Japan, I (get married) _____ .

Rosa: Congratulations!

Steve: Why are you doing that?

Rosa: Steve, that's a terrible thing to say! What's wrong with marriage?

Steve: Nothing. I just think we are too young to get married. I (negative/get

married) _____ until I (be) _____ at least 30 years

old and (have) _____ a good job.

Masa: Steve, when you (meet) _____ the right woman, you (change)

_____ your mind. Just wait and see.

Structured Practice 2   Fill in this time-line about your own future
expectations. Then exchange time-lines with a partner, and discuss them both.
Try to use future time clauses whenever it is possible. Use the information below
as a guide. Also, think of other possible events in your life to put on your time line.
When you finish, write some sentences in the space below the time-line.

MY TIME-LINE
now

English student

Possible events:

learn another language	move to a new home	retire
take a vacation	get married	travel
get a new job	start a business	speak fluent English

Sentences:

Example:

I will speak better English when _I finish my English course._

1. After _____

_____

2. _____

until _____

3. Before _____

_____

4. _____

as soon as _____

Vocabulary   Here are some words that may be useful in your discussion and writing.

to gamble—(verb) to take a risk or chance, especially with money
to play it safe—(idiom) to be cautious
risky—(adjective) dangerous
to fall in love at first sight—(idiom) to feel love for a person at the first moment that you see him/her
to plan—(verb) to carefully arrange a future activity
to leave things to chance—(idiom) to act without any plans
realistic—(adjective) concerned with facts, not influenced by feelings
goal—(noun) one's aim or purpose

Vocabulary Exercise   In the sentences below, fill in the blanks with the correct word or expression from the list above. (You may have to change the form—singular to plural, for example.)

1. It took a long time for Sarah and Sky to fall in love. They did *not* _____ .

2. Sky enjoys taking chances. When he has money, he usually goes to the racetrack and _____ on the horses.

3. Sarah expects her true love to be a perfect person in every way. Sky tells her that her dream is not _____ .

4. Gambling is _____ . You can lose all your money if you are not lucky.

5. Sarah _____ all of her future activities carefully because she doesn't like surprises.

6. Sky believes that he will be successful and happy, even though he never plans anything carefully. He thinks that it's better _____ .

7. You often have to work hard in order to achieve your _____ .

8. Sarah never takes any chances and she doesn't believe in gambling. In other words, she likes _____ .

Discussion and Writing

1. Do you believe in love at first sight?
2. Do you plan your future carefully or do you leave things to chance? Are you cautious like Sarah or a gambler like Sky?
3. Fortune tellers are people who believe they can predict the future through cards, crystal balls, and palm reading. Do you believe that fortune tellers can predict the future? Did you ever go to one?
4. Write a dialog between a fortune teller and a person who wants to hear about his/her future.

10. Parents and Children

Cat's in the Cradle

Grammar Focus   Integration of structures

Song Introduction   The relationship between a parent and a child is a special one. No one has more influence on children than their parents. In this song by Harry Chapin, a busy father tells about his relationship with his son. The words, "cat's in the cradle," "silver spoon," "little boy blue," and "the man in the moon" all come from popular children's nursery rhymes.

Song Task   Listen to the song. As you listen, think about these questions. Underline the parts of the song which contain the necessary information.

1. Why didn't the father hear his son's first words?
2. As a child, was the son angry that his father didn't spend a lot of time with him?
3. How did the father and son relationship change when the son came home from college?
4. As an adult, the son cannot find time to visit his father. What are his reasons?

*Cat's in the Cradle**
by Harry Chapin

1	My child *arrived* just the other day,	was born
2	He came to the world in the usual way.	
3	But there were planes to catch and bills to pay,	
4	He learned to walk while I was away.	
5	And he was talking *'fore* I knew it,	before
6	And as he grew, he'd say,	
7	"I'm going to be like you, Dad.	
8	You know I'm going to be like you."	

CHORUS:

9 And the cat's in the cradle and a silver spoon,
10 Little boy blue and the man in the moon.
11 "When are you coming home, Dad?"
12 "I don't know when.
13 But we'll get together then, son.
14 You know we'll have a good time then."

15 Well, my son turned ten just the other day.
16 He said, "Thanks for the ball, Dad. Come on, let's play.
17 Can you teach me to throw?"
18 I said, "Not today. I've got a lot to do."
19 He said, "That's okay."
20 And then he walked away but his smile never *dimmed*   became weak
21 And said, "I'm going to be like him, yeah.
22 You know, I'm going to be like him."

CHORUS:

23 And the cat's in the cradle and a silver spoon,

24 Little boy blue and the man in the moon.

25 "When are you coming home, Dad?"

26 "I don't know when.

27 But we'll get together then, son.

28 You know we'll have a good time then."

29 Well, he came from college just the other day,

30 So much like a man I just had to say,

31 "Son, I'm proud of you.

32 Can you sit for awhile?"

33 *He shook his head* and he said with a smile,   he said "no"

34 "What I'd really like, Dad, is to borrow the car keys.

35 See you later,

36 Can I have them, please?"

CHORUS:

37 And the cat's in the cradle and a silver spoon,

38 Little boy blue and the man in the moon.

39 "When are you coming home, Son?"

40 "I don't know when.

41 But we'll get together then, Dad.

42 You know we'll have a good time then."

43 Well, *I've long since retired,* my son's moved   I stopped working a long time ago.
    away.

44 I called him up just the other day.

45 I said, "I'd like to see you,

46 If you don't mind."

47 He said, "I'd love to, Dad, if I can find the time.

48 You see, my new job's *a hassle* and the kids *have*   full of problems / are sick with
    the flu.   influenza

49 But it's sure nice talking to you, Dad.

50 It's been sure nice talking to you."

51 And as he hung up the phone,

52 *It occurred to me.*   I realized

53 He'd grown up just like me.

54 My boy was just like me.

CHORUS:

55 And the cat's in the cradle and a silver spoon,
56 Little boy blue and the man in the moon.
57 "When are you coming home, Son?"
58 "I don't know when.
59 But we'll get together then, Dad.
60 We're going to have a good time then."

Song Task   Now write the answers to the questions in complete sentences.

1. Why didn't the father hear his son's first words? _____

_____

_____

2. As a child, was the son angry that his father didn't spend a lot of time with

him? _____

_____

_____

3. How did the father and son relationship change when the son came home

from college? _____

_____

_____

4. As an adult, the son cannot find time to visit his father. What are his reasons?

_____

_____

See also p. 94.

Structured Practice 1   When the son in the song became a father, he started to keep a diary of his baby's growth. Here is a section of that diary. Fill in the blanks with the correct form of the verb in parentheses. Use the following tenses as necessary: simple past, past continuous, simple present, present continuous, and future.

Dear Diary _____ ,

While I (play) _____ with my son yesterday, he (take)

_____ his first steps. At first, he (stand) _____ up and (fall)

_____ down several times. But then he (start) _____ walking across the room. As he (walk) _____ , my wife (come) _____ home from work. I (be) _____ surprised because she (get) _____ home earlier than usual. She usually (work) _____ until 6:00 p.m. We (be) _____ very excited and happy that we (be) _____ both there to see this important event.

After my son (go) _____ to sleep, I (begin) _____ to think about my own childhood and my relationship with my father. I (negative/think) _____ my father (see) _____ me take my first steps. He (be) _____ always busy with work. He (negative/be) _____ a bad father; in fact I (admire) _____ him very much. He often (give) _____ me presents. But he (negative/spend) _____ much time with me.

Now my children (grow up) _____ . They (change) _____ every day. I (spend) _____ as much time with them as possible because I (want) _____ to be closer to them than my father (be) _____ to me.

I (have) _____ a problem now, and I (try) _____ to decide what to do. My boss (offer) _____ me a new job a few days ago. If I (accept) _____ it, I (make) _____ much more money than I (earn) _____ now. There (be) _____ only one problem—I (need) _____ to travel a lot and spend a lot of time in the office. I (negative/have) _____ a lot of time for my family. I (negative/make) _____ a final decision until I (discuss) _____ it with my wife. But I (think) _____ I (know) _____ what she (say) _____ : "Take the job." It (help) _____ my career if I (take) _____ the job, but what about my relationship with my children? (miss) _____ I _____ all the important events in their lives? (be) _____ I _____ like my father?

Structured Practice 2   Complete the sentences below. Some are about the song, and some are general. Write what you think; then compare your sentences with a partner. Use the tenses from the exercise above, as well as the comparative and superlative form of adjectives, as necessary.

1. When the son became a father, he _____

   _____ .

2. The son didn't visit his father because _____

   _____ .

3. The father was away while _____

   _____ .

4. A good parent _____

   _____ .

5. If a father doesn't spend enough time with his son, _____

   _____ .

6. Childhood is the _____ of one's life.

7. Most people don't want to repeat their parents' mistakes. They say, "We won't _____ when _____

   _____ ."

8. In the future, families _____ .

9. The father gave his son presents, but _____

   _____ .

10. Parents always _____

    _____ .

Vocabulary   Here are some words that may be useful in your discussion and writing.

to spend time with someone—(idiom) to pass time with another person
to make time for—(idiom) to set aside special time for someone or something
to bring (someone) up—(verb) to educate and care for children in a family
to raise—(verb) to bring up
upbringing—(noun) training and care of a child
to leave home—(verb) to move out of your parents' home
to affect—(verb) to influence
generation—(noun) all people of about the same age

Vocabulary Exercise   In the sentences below, fill in the blanks with the correct form or expression from the list above. (You may have to change the form—singular to plural, for example.)

1. In the old days, mothers alone were responsible for bringing up their children. The new _____ of parents is trying to share this responsibility.

2. My parents were both very busy people, but they always _____ their children.

3. Because the father in the song was so busy, the mother was completely responsible for the child's _____ .

4. When I was 19, I _____ and rented my own apartment.

5. Many fathers are very busy during the week, so they can only _____ their children on the weekend.

6. In many countries, grandparents help parents to _____ their children.

7. The father in the song didn't make time for his son. This greatly _____ the way the son raised his own child.

8. My parents did not give me a lot of freedom. They _____ very strictly.

Discussion and Writing

1. Retell the story of the song in your own words.
2. At the end of the song, the father says, "My boy is just like me." What does this mean?
3. In your opinion, was the father a good parent? Why?
4. In the United States, it is common for children to leave their parents' home at the age of 18. Is this common in your country?
5. Tell about your relationship with your parents. What do you remember about your relationship with them as a child?
6. In many countries, both mothers and fathers work full-time. How do you think this affects parent-child relationships? Will it have an effect on future generations?

Understanding the Structures

1. **Tennessee Waltz**—Past continuous tense

Understanding the Structures Look at the song again. (Circle) all the verbs after WHEN and draw a box around all the verbs after WHILE. Now complete the chart below.

Time Word   Which tense is used—past or past continuous?

when   _____

while   _____

Forming the past continuous tense:

a. When the subject is I   use *was* (not) + *-ing verb* (present participle)
                        he
                        she
                        it
 Example: I was waltzing....
 When the subject is you   use *were* (not) + *-ing verb* (present participle)
                        we
                        they
 Example: They were dancing....

Lyrics

Tennessee Waltz* by Redd Stewart and Pee Wee King

I was waltzing with my darling
To the Tennessee Waltz,
When an old friend I happened to see.
I introduced him to my darling
And while they were dancing
That friend stole my sweetheart from me.

Yes, I remember the night and the Tennessee Waltz,
Only you know how much I have lost.
When I lost my little darling
The night they were playing
That beautiful Tennessee Waltz.

Yes, I remember the night and the Tennessee Waltz,
Only you know how much I have lost.
When I lost my little darling
The night they were playing
That beautiful Tennessee Waltz.

2. The Marvelous Toy—Past tense (regular and irregular)

Understanding the Structures Read this letter. Then follow the directions below.

Dear Dad,

Yesterday I did something that I want to tell you about. I gave my son the marvelous toy that I received from you 30 years ago. He loved it! He knew right away that it was a special gift. He didn't know what it was, but he started to play with it immediately. He picked it up, studied all its parts, and played with it for hours. He stopped only when he went to sleep.

Thank you again for this wonderful gift—from both of us.

Love,

Dick

1. Underline all the past tense verbs (affirmative and negative) in the letter.
2. With most verbs, we add -*ed* to form the past tense.

   "He started to play with it immediately."
   "He picked it up . . ."
   ". . . and played with it for hours."

   Note: When the verb ends with *e,* just add *d* (for example, *loved*). When the verb ends with consonant + *y,* change the *y* to *i* and add *ed* (for example, *studied*)

3. *Irregular Verbs* Many verbs are irregular in the past tense. They do not end with -*ed.* Here are some examples from the song:

   be—was/were   do—did   know—knew

4. For negatives (except BE and modals), use:

   did not/didn't + base form   "He didn't know what it was."

Lyrics

The Marvelous Toy * by Tom Paxton

When I was just a wee little lad
Full of health and joy
My father homeward came one night
And gave to me a toy.
A wonder to behold it was
With many colors bright

And the moment I laid eyes on it
It became my heart's delight.

CHORUS:
It went "zip" when it moved
And "bop" when it stopped,
"Wrrrrr" when it stood still.
I never knew just what it was
And I guess I never will.

The first time that I picked it up
I had a big surprise
'Cause right on the bottom were two big buttons
That looked like big green eyes.
I first pushed one and then the other,
Then I twisted its lid,
And when I set it down again
Here is what it did.

CHORUS

The years have gone by too quickly it seems,
I have my own little boy
And yesterday I gave to him my marvelous little toy.
His eyes nearly popped right out of his head
And he gave a squeal of glee.
Neither one of us knows just what it is
But he loves it just like me.

It still goes "zip" when it moves
And "bop" when it stops,
"Wrrrrr" when it stands still.
I never knew just what it was
And I guess I never will.

3.   Under the Boardwalk—Prepositions of place

Understanding the Structures   Prepositions are small but important words. Use the picture on p. 83 to help you check your understanding of each preposition of place. Match each item with the sentence that describes it.

_____   1.   The ice cream stand is *on* the boardwalk.

_____   2.   The amusement park is *near* the boardwalk.

_____   3.   The people are lying *under* the boardwalk.

_____   4.   The children are *in* the ocean.

_____   5.   The lifeguard is sitting high *above* the ground.

_____   6.   The child is standing *between* his parents.

_____   7.   The hotel is *at* the end of the boardwalk.

_____   8.   The gas station is *across from* the movie theater.

_____   9.   The Sunshine Motel is *in the middle of* Beach Avenue.

Lyrics

*Under the Boardwalk** by Arthur Resnick and Kenny Young

When the sun beats down and burns the tar up on the roof,
And your shoes get so hot you wish your tired feet were fireproof,
Under the boardwalk, down by the sea,
On a blanket with my baby,
That's where I'll be.

CHORUS:
Under the boardwalk,
Out of the sun,
Under the boardwalk,
We'll be having some fun.
Under the boardwalk,
People walking above,
Under the boardwalk,

We'll be falling in love,
Under the boardwalk, boardwalk.

From the park you hear the happy sounds of the carousel,
You can almost taste the hot dogs and french fries they sell.
Under the boardwalk, down by the sea,
On a blanket with my baby,
That's where I'll be.

CHORUS

Under the boardwalk, down by the sea,
On a blanket with my baby,
That's where I'll be.

CHORUS

4. **Oh, What a Beautiful Mornin'**—Present continuous tense

Understanding the Structures Read this postcard. Then follow the directions below.

Dear Henry,

I am visiting Washington, D.C. with Mel and Paula. We are not wasting any time. We're going to all the sights. Mel is visiting the Science Museum now, and Paula is taking a tour of the White House. This is their first trip to Washington and they are enjoying it very much.

You are planning a vacation to Washington soon, aren't you? It's a great idea!

Take care,
James

Henry Gomez
5 Baker Avenue
Tempe, AZ   85281

1. Look at the postcard above. Underline all the verbs (affirmative and negative).

2. To form the present continuous tense, we use a form of the verb *BE* + *(verb)ING*

   "I *am visiting* Washington, D.C."
   "They *are enjoying* it very much."

3. For negatives, use:

   BE + N'T/NOT + (verb)ING   "We aren't wasting any time."

Lyrics

Oh, What a Beautiful Mornin'* by Richard Rodgers and Oscar Hammerstein II

(Well,) There's a bright golden haze on the meadow,
There's a bright golden haze on the meadow.
The corn is as high as an elephant's eye,
And it looks like it's climbing clear up to the sky.

CHORUS:
(Well,) Oh, what a beautiful mornin',
Oh, what a beautiful day.
I've got a beautiful feeling,
Everything's going my way.

All the cattle are standing like statues,
All the cattle are standing like statues,
They don't turn their heads as they see me ride by,
But a little brown maverick is winking her eye. (She says . . .)

CHORUS:
Oh, what a beautiful mornin', (yeah)
Oh, what a beautiful day. (I want you all to know . . .)
I've got a beautiful feeling,
Everything's going my way. (yeah)

All the sounds of the earth are like music,
All the sounds of the earth are like music.
The breeze is so busy it don't miss a tree,
And an old weeping willow is laughing at me. (She said . . .)

CHORUS:
Oh, what a beautiful mornin', (yeah, yeah)
Oh, what a beautiful day.
I've got a beautiful feeling,
Everything's going my way.
Oh, what a beautiful day.

*OH, WHAT A BEAUTIFUL MORNIN'. Copyright © 1943 by Richard Rodgers and Oscar Hammerstein, II. Copyright Renewed Williamson Music Inc., Owner of publication and allied rights for the Western Hemisphere and Japan (administered by Chappell and Co., Inc.). International Copyright Secured. ALL RIGHTS RESERVED. Used by Permission.

5. **Little Boxes**—Simple present tense

Understanding the Structures

"Your brother studies hard. He doesn't waste his time. He follows the rules and accomplishes his goals. You stay home and paint those silly pictures. Do you want to be poor all your life?"

"We only want the best for you but you don't listen to us. All of your friends go to school or work. They don't paint. We do not understand you. Why don't children listen to their parents?"

"I love art. I want to be a painter. I don't want anything else."

1. Look at the statements in the dialog. Underline all the verbs (some are affirmative and some are negative).
2. a. With most subjects, we use the BASE FORM of the verb in the simple present tense.

   "I *love* art"
   "You *stay* home"
   "We *want* the best for you"
   "They *go* to school"

   For negatives, use *DO NOT + BASE FORM:* "We *do not understand* you."

   b. With the 3rd person singular (he, she, it) we use the *BASE FORM of the verb + S.*

   "He *works* hard."

   For negatives, we use *DOES NOT + BASE FORM:* "He *does not waste* his time."

   Note: A. *Irregular Verbs*
   HAVE—3rd person form = *has*
   DO—3rd person form = *does* (pronunciation /dəz/)
   B. *Spelling Rules*
   When the verb ends with a vowel (except "e"), sh, ss, ch, or x, *add -ES.*
   When the verb ends with consonant + y, *change the "y" to "i" and add -ES.*

Lyrics

*Little Boxes** by Malvina Reynolds

Little boxes on the hillside
Little boxes made of ticky tacky
Little boxes, little boxes
Little boxes all the same.
There's a green one and a pink one
And a blue one and a yellow one,
And they're all made out of ticky tacky
And they all look just the same.

And the people in the houses
All go to the university
And they all get put in boxes,
Little boxes all the same.
And there's doctors and there's lawyers
And business executives
And they're all made out of ticky tacky
And they all look just the same.

And they all play on the golf course
And drink their martini dry
And they all have pretty children
And the children go to school.
And the children go to summer camp
And then to the university
And they all get put in boxes
And they all come out the same.

And the boys go into business
And marry and raise a family
And they all get put in boxes
Little boxes all the same.
There's a green one and a pink one
And a blue one and a yellow one
And they're all made out of ticky tacky
And they all look just the same.

Little Boxes. Words and music by Malvina Reynolds. © 1962 Schroder Music Co. Used by permission. All rights reserved.

6. **My Love**—Comparative and superlative of adjectives

Understanding the Structures Look at the song again. List the adjectives from the song that are comparatives and the adjectives that are superlatives.

Comparatives	Superlatives
1. _____	1. _____
2. _____	2. _____
3. _____	3. _____
4. _____	
5. _____	

1. All of the adjectives above are one-syllable words. When an adjective is only one syllable, we just add -er to compare it with something else (*example:* wider than . . .). To talk about a unique quality we use "*the -est*" (*example:* the widest).
2. When an adjective has two or more syllables we use "more + adjective" to form the comparative (*example:* more difficult than) and "the most + adjective" to form the superlative (*example:* the most difficult).
3. When an adjective ends with "y" (*example:* pretty), change the "y" to "i" and add -er or -est (*example:* prettier than, the prettiest).
4. Some adjectives have irregular comparative and superlative forms. *Example:*

	Comparative	Superlative
good –	better	the best
bad –	worse	the worst

Lyrics

*My Love** by Tony Hatch

CHORUS:
My love is warmer than the warmest sunshine,
Softer than a sigh,
My love is deeper than the deepest ocean
Wider than the sky.
My love is brighter than the brightest star
That shines every night above,
And there is nothing in this world that can ever change my love.

Something happened to my heart
The day that I met you,

*MY LOVE. Words and music by TONY HATCH. © copyright 1965 by WELBECK MUSIC, Ltd. London, England. Sole selling Agent, DUCHESS MUSIC CORPORATION (MCA), New York, N.Y. for USA and Canada. USED BY PERMISSION. ALL RIGHTS RESERVED.

Something that I never felt before
You are always on my mind
No matter what I do,
And every day it seems I want you more.

CHORUS

Once I thought that love was meant
For anyone else but me,
Once I thought you'd never come my way
Now it only goes to show
How wrong we all can be,
For now I have to tell you every day.

CHORUS

7. I'm Gonna Sit Right Down and Write Myself a Letter—
Future tense

Understanding the Structures Predictions, promises, statements of intention, and statements of future action are all very close in meaning. Some people use *will* and *going to* for all functions.

In this exercise, some sentences are clearly one function only. Others may have more than one possible function.

Look at each sentence with *will* and *going to*. With a partner, decide which function *you* think the verb shows in each sentence. Here are the four functions:

1. intention/plan
2. promise/willingness
3. prediction
4. general future

Function

A: Please remember to call me tomorrow.

B: Don't worry! *I will.* 1. *promise*

A: Remember. *I'm not going to be* at home. 2. _____

I'll be at work all day. 3. _____

B: Okay, okay. *I'll call* you at work. 4. _____

A: Oh, I know *you'll forget.* You always forget to 5. _____

call me.

B: I *will call* you at work tomorrow. I promise! 6. _____

A: Don't call after 5 p.m. I *won't be* there after 5. 7. _____

B: Okay, *I'll call* you between 3:30 and 4:30 p.m. 8. _____

A: Great. *I'll talk* to you then. 9. _____

Lyrics

*I'm Gonna Sit Right Down and Write Myself a Letter** by F. Ahlert and J. Young

I'm gonna sit right down and write myself a letter (yes, yes)
And make believe it came from you (you, I love you, love you)
I'm gonna write words oh, so sweet,
They're gonna knock me off these (size 12) feet,
A lot of kisses on the bottom (kisses on the bottom, yes)
I'll be glad I got 'em.
I'm gonna smile and say "Gee, I hope you're feeling better."
(Better, better, it's a killer)
And close "with love" the way you do (you do.)
I'm gonna sit right down and write myself a postcard,
(I gotta save some money, you know, yes)
And make believe, make believe,
I'm gonna make believe it came from you.

8.   Tie A Yellow Ribbon 'Round the Old Oak Tree—
Real conditional

Understanding the Structures   In the song, Vingo states his plan for the future. He says, "If I don't see a yellow ribbon 'round the old oak tree, I'll stay on the bus. . . ."

What tense is used in the "if" clause? _____

What tense is used in the "result" clause? _____

The real conditional tells about two future events. One event is the result of the other and both events are possible. In the result clause, we often use the modals *will, can,* or *may* with the main verb.

For example:

First Future Event	*Second Future Event (Result)*
If Vingo sees a yellow ribbon around the tree . . .	a. he will get off the bus. (it's certain that this will happen)
	b. he may cry from happiness. (it's possible this will happen)
	c. he can live with his family again. (he has the ability to do this)

*I'M GONNA SIT RIGHT DOWN AND WRITE MYSELF A LETTER. Words by Joe Young. Music by Fred E. Ahlert. © 1935 Chappell & Co., Inc. © Renewed 1963 Rytvoc, Inc. International Copyright Secured. All rights Reserved. Used by Permission. Copyright © 1935 by DeSylva, Brown & Henderson, Inc. Copyright Renewed—Assigned to Fred Ahlert Music Corp, Pencil Mark Music & Rytvoc Inc., for the U.S.A. All rights for the world outside the U.S.A. controlled by Chappell & Co., Inc. International Copyright Secured. ALL RIGHTS RESERVED. Used by Permission.

Note: *Will, may,* and *can* are modal auxiliary verbs. A verb following the modal *will, may,* or *can* is always in the base form.

Examples: he will get off
he may cry
he can live

Lyrics

*Tie a Yellow Ribbon 'Round the Old Oak Tree** by L. Russell Brown

I'm coming home, I've done my time.
Now I've got to know what is and isn't mine.
If you received my letter
Telling you I'd soon be free,
Then you'll know just what to do
If you still want me,
If you still want me.

CHORUS:
Oh, tie a yellow ribbon 'round the old oak tree.
It's been three long years.
Do you still want me? (still want me)
If I don't see a ribbon 'round the old oak tree,
I'll stay on the bus, forget about us,
Put the blame on me,
If I don't see a yellow ribbon 'round the old oak tree.

Bus driver, please look for me
'Cause I couldn't bear to see what I might see.
I'm really still in prison,
And my love, she holds the key.
A simple yellow ribbon's
What I need to set me free.
I wrote and told her, "Please . . ."

CHORUS

Now, the whole damn bus is cheering
And I can't believe I see
A hundred yellow ribbons 'round the old oak tree!
(I'm coming home, um hum.
Tie a ribbon . . .)

9. **I'll Know**—Future time clauses

Understanding the Structures   Look at the song and the time-line below. Complete the sentences according to the information in the song.
Sarah and Sky's Time-line:

before   when / as   after
                               as soon as

until
till then

Example:

When *Sarah meets her true love, she will marry him.*

　　　　　　　　future time clause　　　　　　　　　　　main clause

1. As soon as _____

2. _____ until _____

3. _____ before _____

4. When _____

5. _____ after _____

Note: The time clause can come in the beginning or the middle of the sentence without a change in meaning. Look at the example sentence again:

　"When Sarah meets her true love, she will marry him."

We can also say:

　"Sarah will marry her true love when she meets him."

Notice that we use a comma after the future time clause only when the time clause comes first in the sentence.

Lyrics

I'll Know* by Frank Loesser

　Sky: I'm not interested in what he will not be. I'm interested in what he will be.
Sarah: Well, don't worry, I'll know.

*I'LL KNOW by Frank Loesser from *Guys and Dolls*. © 1950 FRANK MUSIC CORP. © Renewed 1978 FRANK MUSIC CORP. International Copyright Secured. All Rights Reserved. Used by Permission. "Excerpt from musical play 'Guys and Dolls'; Used by permission. © Copyright, 1951 by Jo Swerling, Abe Burrows and Frank Loesser. © Copyright Renewed, 1979 by Jo Swerling, Abe Burrows and Frank Loesser. All Rights Reserved.

For I've imagined every bit of him, from his strong moral fiber to the wisdom in his head, to the homey aroma of his pipe.

Sky: You have wished yourself a real dumb character, a square-thinking, pencil-pushing type.

Sarah: Yes, and I shall meet him when the time is right.

Sky: You've got your guy all figured out, huh?

Sarah: I have.

Sky: Including what he smokes, all figured out.

Sarah: All figured out.
I'll know when my love comes along,
I won't take a chance.
I'll know he'll be just what I need,
Not some fly-by-night Broadway romance.

Sky: And you'll know at a glance by the crease in his pants.

Sarah: Yes, I'll know by that calm, steady voice,
Those feet on the ground.
I'll know as I run to his arms
That at last I've come home safe and sound.
And till then I shall wait,
And till then I'll be strong
For I'll know when my love comes along.

Sky: No, no, no. You're talking about love. You can't dope it like that. What are you picking—a guy or a horse?

Sarah: Oh, I wouldn't expect a gambler to understand.

Sky: Would you like to hear how a gambler feels about the big love deal?

Sarah: No.

Sky: Well, I'll tell you.
Mine will come as a surprise to me.
Mine I leave to chance and chemistry.

Sarah: Chemistry?

Sky: Yeah, chemistry.
I'll know when my love comes along
I'll know then and there.
I'll know at the sight of her face,
How I care, how I care, how I care.
And I'll stop and I'll stare.
And I'll know long before we can speak
And I'll know in my heart,
And I'll know, and I won't ever ask
Am I right? Am I wise? Am I smart?
And I'll stop, and I'll stare
At that face in the throng.
Yes, I'll know when my love comes along,
I'll know when my love comes along.

10. Cat's in the Cradle—
Review of structures in preceding units

Lyrics

*Cat's in the Cradle** by Harry Chapin

My child arrived just the other day,
He came to the world in the usual way.
But there were planes to catch and bills to pay,
He learned to walk while I was away.
And he was talking 'fore I knew it,
And as he grew, he'd say,
"I'm going to be like you, Dad.
You know I'm going to be like you."

CHORUS:
And the cat's in the cradle and a silver spoon,
Little boy blue and the man in the moon.
"When are you coming home, Dad?"
"I don't know when.
But we'll get together then, son.
You know we'll have a good time then."

Well, my son turned ten just the other day.
He said, "Thanks for the ball, Dad. Come on, let's play.
Can you teach me to throw?"
I said, "Not today. I've got a lot to do."
He said, "That's okay."
And then he walked away but his smile never dimmed
And said, "I'm going to be like him, yeah.
You know, I'm going to be like him."

CHORUS:
And the cat's in the cradle and a silver spoon,
Little boy blue and the man in the moon.
"When are you coming home, Dad?"
"I don't know when.
But we'll get together then, son.
You know we'll have a good time then."

Well, he came from college just the other day,
So much like a man I just had to say,
"Son, I'm proud of you.
Can you sit for awhile?"

*CAT'S IN THE CRADLE by Harry Chapin. © Story Songs Ltd., 1974. All Rights Reserved. Used by Permission. International Copyright Secured.

He shook his head and he said with a smile,
"What I'd really like, Dad, is to borrow the car keys.
See you later,
Can I have them, please?"

CHORUS:
And the cat's in the cradle and a silver spoon,
Little boy blue and the man in the moon.
"When are you coming home, Son?"
"I don't know when.
But we'll get together then, Dad.
You know we'll have a good time then."

Well, I've long since retired, my son's moved away.
I called him up just the other day.
I said, "I'd like to see you,
If you don't mind."
He said, "I'd love to, Dad, if I can find the time.
You see, my new job's a hassle and the kids have the flu.
But it's sure nice talking to you, Dad.
It's been sure nice talking to you."
And as he hung up the phone,
It occurred to me.
He'd grown up just like me.
My boy was just like me.

CHORUS:
And the cat's in the cradle and a silver spoon,
Little boy blue and the man in the moon.
"When are you coming home, Son?"
"I don't know when.
But we'll get together then, Dad.
We're going to have a good time then."